MARIA
BREAKS HER SILENCE
——— POEMS ———

NANCY MATTSON

July 1990

For the Murphys –
a story from the
Canadian prairies – hope
you enjoy it!

Nancy Mattson

COTEAU

Cover painting "Rollande" (1929) by Prudence Heward, collection of the National Gallery of Canada. Used by permission of the Heward family, Montréal.
Book design by Joyce Sotski.
Author photograph by Peter Sutherland Photography, Edmonton.
Typeset by Publication Associates (Regina) Limited.
Printed by Hignell Printing, Winnipeg.
Printed and bound in Canada.
The publisher gratefully acknowledges the financial assistance of the Saskatchewan Arts Board, the Canada Council and the Department of Communications in the publication of this book.

with the assistance of the
Saskatchewan
Arts Board

Canadian Cataloguing in Publication Data

Mattson, Nancy, 1947-

Maria breaks her silence

(The Wood Mountain series ; 9)
Poems.
ISBN: 0-919926-92-4 (bound) ; 0-919926-93-2 (pbk).

1. Finnish Canadians - Poetry*. I. Title. II. Series.

PS8576.A88M3 1989   C811'.54   C89-098001-2
PR9199.3.M388M3 1989

coteau books

Editorial Office:
Suite 209, 1945 Scarth St.
Regina, Saskatchewan
S4P 2H2
(306) 352-5346

Distribution Office:
Box 239, Sub. #1
Moose Jaw, Saskatchewan
S6H 5V0
(306) 693-5212

For my mother, Anne Nordlund Mattson; my daughter, Leah Schelstraete; and in memory of my grandmothers, Anna Mäntysaari Mattson and Olga Forsberg Nordlund.

CONTENTS———————

PREFATORY NOTE

Maria was born in 1846 in Finland, and again in 1983 in my Edmonton imagination. I had spent two years as editor and researcher of a history of New Finland, Saskatchewan, where my grandparents homesteaded and my parents were born. It was an exhilarating and exhausting process, recording the official history of the place where I spent all my joyous childhood summers. After the history book went to press, poems began appearing in my notebooks about a particular woman whose story intrigued me; she began to take over part of my consciousness. I discovered her by piecing together genealogies, and found out a little more about her by writing to one of her granddaughters. Like so many women and men who left no diaries or letters, who were too busy or too poor to sit for photographs or portraits, Maria exists for the historian only as a paragraph of demographic data. But between the lines of official history are the inner lives of ordinary people who struggled and laughed and gossiped and worked and loved. The Maria in these poems is one such woman. I have taken liberties with some of the few known details of her life; the cultural context is accurate, based on experience and research. Maria Nahkala Kautonen Lauttamus. Maria maiden name unknown. Maria everywoman.

WRITING

a poem about a famous man
is one thing:
    Socrates
    Blake
    Picasso

but to speak about a woman
whose voice was lost
as she shifted
    continents
    languages
    husbands
    names
one dying into another

whose letters were lost in
    oceans
    furrows
    decades

whose thoughts were lost in
    sewing
    washing
    making do

from under a tangle of genealogies
    rosebushes
    cloudberries
    nettles

your voice, maria, whispering
growing strong

FINLAND

MARIA LEARNS THE ART OF BAKING

The place to learn the art of baking bread
is not at the end of your mother-in-law's tongue
but in your own home
instructed every Thursday by the town expert
the baker Kautonen with his sincere smile
Let the neighbour ladies peer
through their lace curtains
when Kautonen comes to my door
delivering his specialty loaves
Let all the women of Kauhava
sneer under lace in their pews
when Matt and I come to church
and Kautonen sits on the pulpit side
Even Mrs. Petlä cannot deny
my basic rye loaf is improving every week
under the training of Kautonen
    flour under his fingernails
    dough in the knuckle-grooves
    both of us in aprons
Though I still need help with the wheat bread
and we haven't even tried
the braided *pulla*, the prune pasties

MARIA LEARNS RESENTMENT

From the last batch of yeast buns
that David baked in her kitchen
before he sneaked away from Kauhava
Maria gave twelve fresh to her husband

but wrapped the thirteenth in a white cloth
woven fine on her mother's loom
        linen edged in lace
        embroidered with snowdrops
        never a knot

put the wrapped loaf
into her own oval basket
fashioned as a girl
from the bark of a fresh birch
        with a deft clasp
        never a seam

hid the basket in her father's chest
of smooth white birch
        with carved handles
        mortised corners
        never a nail

After sweaty rituals with her husband
Maria waited until he snored
washed herself with scalded water
rocked herself dry
naked beside the cast-iron stove

Inside the closed chest
under layers of birch and linen
aromas of yeast, cardamom, cloves
hardened to a fist

MATT BREAKS HIS SILENCE

Matt has not spoken in four days.
On the first, Maria respected his silence
offered hopeful glances to his glares
waited her turn. Simply waited.

On the second, she sparrowed her words
as she hopped from stove to sideboard
his woman, making his meals on time
serving them up with gossip and plans
balancing towards him on the edge of her chair.

On the third, the pleading began
small at first, then growing larger and more
embarrassing
like a pregnant woman's belly
swollen with purple stretch marks
and a sore-apple navel.
She thrust herself at him.
He turned his head.

On the fourth day.
She bars his exit from their bedroom.
Fills the doorway with her need.
Acknowledge me.
The fist arrives.
She is grateful.
Tastes his knuckles.
Hears the force of the backhand to her ear.
Welcomes his curse.

MARIA MAKES SOUP

Today we will choose a rooster, Maria
for tonight's supper
come to the chicken coop with me
pick a fine rooster
I will hold his legs
you will squeeze his neck
like you wring those scalding towels

Don't make me do it, Matt
that's your job
killing chickens

It's time you learned—
maybe you can lop off
his head with an axe
but I won't hold him down
you might miss and split my thumb
Which will it be:
whetted axe-blade
or hands around his neck?

Matt watched, breathed on her neck:
Woman, feeble-handed one
feeble-minded too

She choked the rooster
swallowing gravel and mucus
hands and forearms muscled
from years of pulling
rubbery teats of cows

Nodules of gristle
formed at the base of her skull
two hard little blood-rocks
formed in the veins
crept up to the temples

All day in the kettle
the rooster meat softened
in onion juices, carrot and cabbage

At supper she could not swallow
or look at Matt
devouring his soup
asking for more

MARIA HANGS OUT THE WASH

Maria ties her clothespin bag
a modified apron with a pouch for wooden washboys
around her waist the weight of the pouch pulls
in at her waist, defines her hips
the pouch is a lumpy canvas udder
swinging against her skirt
loose between her thighs.
She balances the bassinet
of wet laundry on one hip—
as she walks to the clothesline
her rear end wants to sway
she swishes her tail
to keep away the flies

Maria and the cows stare at each other
the cows chew from side to side
jaws cudding impassive
like the old women at the sewing circle
mouthing their gums
sucking their coffee sugar.
But these are young lady cows
they grind their teeth modestly
mouths closed, lips relaxed
>   *(she grinds her teeth at night*
>   *stares at Matt, lips tight*
>   *when he tells her she is a cow*
>   *a slovenly cow with hanging tits)*

Cows are so delicate, she thinks
their earflaps finely modelled
white powder on their eyelashes
smooth fur in spotted patterns
stretched over elegant hipbones
she likes the way they place each foot
graceful on the grassy hill
their hoofs are satin toe shoes
their tails swish like tutus
of Russian ballerinas

The cows watch Maria build a fence of clothing
pinning flaps of fabric on the line
coloured and white, corner to corner
dipping into her pouch
for washboys to straddle the clothes

Old Kammokki snorts over the hill
his heavy sac swinging between his hind legs
surveys his cows with fond complacency
they pirouette against a backdrop of poplars
"Sway your flanks, cowdancers,
lift up your skirts hindmost to his nose
like shameless dancehall floozies.
Dance around together, hem in old Kammokki
with a circle of *pylly* so delicious
that his muscular tongue will drool
and his bullrod sigh in despair
at servicing so many sugarplum fairies."

Kammokki chooses one cow for an *yksi-kaksi*
nips her softly along her side
licks and laps as she pulls her tail aside
when he slides in his rod
they moo in a mutual cowgroan

Maria claps and grins
they are so free and spotted
her clothes are blowing fresh on the line

She hears the sound of Matt's horses
soon he'll be pulling into the yard
            (he came at her last night
            when she was half-asleep
            ploughed into her
            like a seed drill into a dry furrow)

She unties her clothespin bag
drops it in the empty basket
goes into the house to make his lunch

MARIA DOES THE IRONING

It isn't a task, it is ritual:
the five black irons
lined up at the back of the stove
like sleeping babies on a mattress
and there's something satisfying
in the click of the handle
every time she picks up a fresh iron
then the gentle heavy rattle
as she pulls the iron over sheets and pillowslips
that's where she always begins

But then the decision:
do Matt's things now
or delay them till afternoon
nursing her reluctance
letting it heat up slowly
burning away contentment

Pick up the first shirt, Maria
remember how far it is from his sweat:
lye soap, boiling water
purifying wind

Start with the collar, think of his neck:
let the iron stay on the wrinkles
just until you start to smell the singe

She shifts the fabric on the padded board
clicks into the hottest iron
sears it into the armpits
(carefully follows the seams)
turns the shirt to the broad expanse of back
where the cloth has been stretched by his shoulders
pains will come to him later, unexpectedly
as he ploughs the field, sun on his back

After his clothes are folded, stacked, buried
she takes a small dress from the basket:
the iron bumps over embroidered knots and petals
renews the smoothness of the bodice
runs over clever pockets hidden in skirt seams
makes the ruffles stand up
like rows of starched petunias

LIISA DRAWS A PICTURE

This is my own father, *minun isä*
he is rowing away in a boat
like the old man at the lake

> he fills the pail with perch
> yesterday he gave me three
> I don't like porridge for supper
> black bugs float in the milk

Äiti says my father's boat has no oars
I will start again, draw a wind boat
with a white sheet to catch the wind

> When *Äiti* hangs the sheets outside
> they flap like big wings
> the wind twists them around the line
> crows are noisy when they laugh

These are my father's eyes, *isän silmät*
black and hard like coal
I have black eyes too

> Tiina's eyes are light and soft
> like my own blue sweater
> *Isä* carved her a wooden cradle
> it cries when I rock her to sleep

Rain is streaming down my father's face
a fierce grey bird flies out of the storm
swoops and knocks him down

       Isto pushed me into a rose bush
       called me a gypsy bum-child
       my blue sweater got ripped on a branch
       Isto laughed like a crow

The storm is gone now, the stars are out
these are the dancing women of the North
flashing their skirts round Väinämöinen's sickle

       I hear my father's mandolin
       my mother's song, like crying
       I will go outside now
       to catch her some fireflies

TIETÄJÄ: ONE WHO KNOWS

When Paavo, the seasoned lumberman
strikes his foot with an axe
the devil's axe seeking a tree root
finding instead Paavo's ankle
through layers of boot and heavy sock

When Paavo's blood is soaking earth and wood
his eyes swimming
in branches and clouds
what can he do but send for Maria,
village blood-stopper?
Run, little helper
to the cottage of the *tietäjä*
we all despise her except in distress
now that her husband has left her

Three heavy lumbermen carry Paavo
a log filled with pain
his leg wrapped in sodden shirts
to Maria's kitchen
her children standing around

She unwraps his foot
dips her hands in the stream of blood
seeks out the edges of his wound
presses the slippery flesh together
        skin to skin
threads the rivers of blood
        vein to vein
lifts her head to Ahto
utters these words:

        Blood, blood, become a wall
        thicken, thicken, like a fence
        stay, stay, behind my hands
        stop, stop, beneath my thumbs!

16

As Maria chants what she knows, chanting softly
the lumberman Paavo, fearful as a wounded bear
falls quiet under her hands
When the sun falls, his blood sleeps
dries in thick threads and wooden scabs

Maria rises, her hair matted
blood crusting on her arms
she hears his breathing, listens
to the cracked whispers of blood

MICHIGAN

MARIA READS THE LETTER

She never wanted to be a foreigner
a gypsy singing her children to sleep
in a language everyone stares at
here in America
on the train to a place
her tongue can't pronounce—
Ishpeming, Michigan—
a mining town where a stranger lives
her husband, lost for dead

She unfolds his letter again
remembering the day
it was first delivered:
black scratches from a man
with a black heart
      a liar's heart
      a wicked heart
      a gypsy heart:
      mustalainen sydän
      ilkeänlainen sydän

Go away from me, wicked gypsy!
I wish you drowned
in the bottom of a well
crushed by rocks and spat upon
and now you betray me
alive in my hands
your bitter scrawls on thin paper
I will crush you very small
      burn you in the stove
      watch your ashes float to the ceiling

But a letter comes a long way
over a wide ocean
I wonder
what you are doing in America

Ishpeming, America
March 4, 1886

My dear Maria,

I have no right to send you a message. Please if you
will forgive me. I long to see my daughters again,
making sentences in the language of my own
boyhood in Suomi, growing tall with braided hair the
color of the wheat.

I myself have been sailing on the ocean with rough
men, wickeder than I am wicked. But I never take the
drink. I have worked on the Iron Range, lonely in the
pit, with many fellows covered in red dust. The earth
is robbed of its ore, my leather purse is sticking out
with money. It is for you I only save. The pit is very
wide and deep.

It was a bad man I have been, now my heart of stone
is softer away from you. I regret many of the actions,
will you again consider to be my true wife? Will you
bring my children, abandoned for a long time ago?
There is a big house here for you, you may forgive
me, I was ill with yellow fever. A man of God on the
island Cuba put oil on my head and made his hand
into a cross. He prayed for me not in Finnish, not in
English, not again in Spanish, very old chanting
words. My life was saved, I slept and waked and saw
my errors. Come to America I humbly request. The
streets, I am honest, are not of the gold but the red
dust of the iron. It is rich and I am free.

You will find in the folds passage money for you and
the children to America, New York, and also by train
fare where I am in Ishpeming. You may not choose to
arrive, then use the money for your own self, sorrow
money for three years I am absent. However I beg you
will send your reply like a bird across the ocean my
heart flies to you.

Your husband,
Matti

MARIA'S HOUSE

I've bought a house for you, Maria
here in Ishpeming, a fine house
a big house, *varmasti isotalo*
bigger than your father's

He led her up the steps
across the verandah
held open the door
took her hand
to show her the rooms

She saw the long dining table
such a big table for a family of five
with long benches on either side
the two big stoves in the kitchen
and knew the house was big for a reason

Many rooms upstairs to shelter men
many plates in the cupboard to feed men
miners, loggers, anyone who could pay
drunkards, laggards, anyone who could drag
his feet up the stairs
anyone who could gamble, argue, swear
and pay his weekly board and room

Not like her father's house in Kauhava
with its many bedrooms for guests
many children, many servants
here she was to be the servant
to many strangers
paljon muukalaisia
cooking men's meals
washing men's coveralls
stripping men's beds
washing men's floors with lye soap

I'll fix you some coffee
you look tired after your long journey
sit down in this rocking chair
I'm so glad you're here, Maria

MARIA LEARNS THE SOURCE OF BEAUTY

At last Maria can use her crochet hook
instead of the knitting needles
which grow from her fingers by day

Everyone is safe now, asleep
has mittens for the winter
one pair each and a spare
she's given them intricate patterns for Sundays
solid colors for routine wear

She uses her midnight time by the stove
to treat herself to gloves with lacy fingers
to decorate her fingers, not protect them

Webbing the flowers, she looks forward
to objections by her husband
relishes his outrage at her waste of sleep
her devotion to white gloves
that do nothing more than expose
her fingers to the Michigan winter

In the corner above the stove, she admires
a delicate white spider dangling
from its own thread

MARIA TELLS HER DREAM

She does not choose to dream
about the corpse of an ancient *mummu*
laid out in dreary lace
frowning with her skin
in death as in life

Yet when the galvanized tub overturns
pouring ice water into the coffin
she pities the wrist that trembles

She does not choose to recount
in the middle of the night
how she wiped the body dry
combed the scissored hair behind the ears
asked the *mummu* if she wanted rouge

Yet when Matt wakes up
she tells him the *mummu* answered
you know I want to be natural
in death as in life
the words came slow and soft
she spoke in sentences

He answers nothing when she explains
how the *mummu* reassured her
it was all right to die
and she was forgiven
for wanting her husband
dead

WIDOWS

Last week Amanda came to visit
told how her husband died
blasted clean away
in a coal mine explosion out west.
Maria is listening, recasting:
that's how Matti died
crushed in a copper mine at Calumet
The women commiserate.
Maria wonders at Amanda's tears.

Today the widow Lydia comes for coffee
sucks sugar, mourns for her husband
who died feverish in her arms.

When Matti was sick
Maria bathed his swollen cheeks
stroked his wooden fingers.
Pulling at her, he whispered
"Do not kill me, Maria."
His fingers crushed her wrists.
The women remember.
Maria tries for tears.

MARIA CRIES

Tell the truth, Maria,
it's all over now
        I covered my ears
he was cold
he hurt you
I saw you with him
your lowered eyes
swallowed words
I couldn't speak then
        I had no tears at the service
It's a cruel death
not even he deserved it
crushed by rocks
the copper shaft his grave
        Maybe I would have cried
        if I'd had a body

Let me hold you

        When I went to the mine that night
        all the wives were crying
        except for me
        I covered my ears

        I went to the cave-in
        the rocks were massive
        I leaned against a boulder
        told him I was sorry
        the boulder rolled away
        all boulders rolled away
        and out of a staring hole
        a thin woman emerged
        crawling on stones

I felt my veins and marrow
slowly fill with tepid water
the first trickles
made my body ache
now I am swelling
with thick colostrum, milk, blood

Cradle me, it hurts to be born

MARIA VISITS HILJA

David who?

Kautonen, do you know him? We got a letter from
him this morning. Oh, it was a good one. I sure miss
that chuckle; his letters are always a treat. He has a
way with words, that man, and he's . . .
    Do I know him?

up north now, homesteading—some place in Canada.
I can't imagine David settling down, such a wanderer.
He was trying to persuade Arvo to come, there's a lot
of land up there. But there's no question, now that he's
pit boss. Anyway, my sister's here now, and she . . .
    miss that chuckle

Did you know she married Eino—remember that
swarthy one, always organizing meetings at the
Temperance Hall? A real talker, but too intense for
my liking. But then I didn't marry him, she did. A
surprising thing happened at the ceremony . . .
    such a wanderer

She met him at Järvenpää's boardinghouse. Oh, she's
glad to get out of there. That old woman Järvenpää
she's a real slave driver. Not like you, Maria, yours is
the best boardinghouse in town. Can you give me the
recipe for that rhubarb . . .
    but then I didn't marry him

I'm worried about that sister of mine. Eino's quite a
troublemaker, always stirring up trouble at the mine.
Arvo's real disgusted with him. Last time they came
over for supper—I made a nice ham and everything—
they argued so much the children ran upstairs. My
sister was crying, it was . . .
    a way with words, that man

These men and their tempers! But we always seem to
marry them. I wonder how David ever stayed single.
Now there's a smooth one, should have been in politics,
the way he could settle people down. It was the way he
talked—a joke here and there, stroke down their fur . . .
    it was the way he talked

He had a way with women, too. Many a girl in
Ishpeming set her sights on him. Just one dance and
he'd break their hearts. But he never treated them
rough, always the gentleman, not like some men. I
like to dance myself, mind you . . .
     break their hearts

He really liked women, even the ones that weren't so
pretty, made them feel like he took them serious. He
even used to talk to me, not gossip and all that
women talk, but really deep, you know what I mean?
He turned some wheels in this old head of mine. He
listened too, even when I got carried away. Arvo's
always telling me to be quiet—"*Ole hiljaa!*" he says.
I get so I can't . . .
     always the gentleman

I think David just liked people—they gathered around
him like cattle at a salt-lick. I can't imagine him all
by himself up there. Arvo said he had a sweetheart in
the old country, but I never heard him mention her.
Here, let me get that letter. He's got a way with
words, and such a beautiful hand.

CROSSINGS

Here on this blunted border
between snow and snow
she is crossing blind
a crone clicks
her teeth on the tracks

She remembers another crossing

a rope thick as a woman's
wrist cut through
by salt scissor wind
moonlight a midwife
ship adrift

She tightens her belt

around the sharp stone
of a wizened berry
the withered grief of leaving home
the train slows down
stops for no reason

She hears through the steam

her daughters' cries, "*Maa maa*"
her body their only country
she settles their heads
on her empty womb
the train pulses forward
from darkness to darkness

NEW FINLAND
(UUSI SUOMI)

DAVID'S HOUSE

Welcome to my bachelor's den
minun poikatalo, a poor place indeed
to bring a lovely woman
and her lovely daughters
but in the spring
I will build us a new house—
make sure you greet the *kotihenki*
as you enter

Cold and silent
from the long sleigh trip
Liisa and Tiina find their voices
thaw them out:

> *Äiti,* why is it so dark in here?
> I feel like I'm in a bear's den
> I think it's a tree hollow
> and we're squirrels
> No, it's a cave,
> we're deep inside a copper mine
> Maybe it's a bear's stomach
> and he's growling
> I'm hungry
> I'm hungry

Isä Karhu has baked fresh bread for you
here is cheese, saskatoon preserves
he slices the bread with a hand-made knife
spider-flowers on the blade

As the girls eat, they eye their mother
eye this strange man
fire crackles in their eyes

Liisa and Tiina pull on their nightdresses
unbraid and brush their hair
whisper questions:

Who is that man?
An old friend, my dears.
Is he our uncle?
Not an uncle, he'll be your stepfather.
Where is this place?
Assiniboia, Canada.
Kyllä! Miksi? Missä? Mitä?
You get to bed now.

She blows out the lamp.

MARIA SHOWS DAVID HER PHOTOGRAPHS

This is a picture of my only son
conceived in a truce
a temporary love
the closest I ever got to Matt

I was afraid to see him again in America
but he had changed
said he confronted the *aaveet*
the evil spirits that had tormented him

Once in a storm at sea
he was alone on watch
a large grey bird flew from the thunder
circled him, screaming
when he killed the bird
he was left unconscious on the deck
nearly drowned by the torrents

Another time, in a fever
the *aave* sat on his chest
a black lizard
staring into his eyes
Matt had no strength to resist
a holy man sent it away

The final time was in the mine
the *aave* crawled out of the red dust
clutched his leg and pulled him down
he struggled and killed it with a pick-axe

This is the way he told it
he had the stories all worked out—
who was I to deny them?
I was grateful he was healed
quiet and thoughtful
as I had never seen him
We had nearly two years of peace
conceived a son and called him Eric

When our son died of consumption
Matt went down again
I became the *aave*
he blamed me for Eric's death
called me a witch
said I had contaminated him
with my milk

David touches her hand

DAVID BREAKS HIS SILENCE

1

The day before I left
I performed the ceremony of lead
melted the metal
poured it on snow
a ship emerged
I wrapped it in a coarse handkerchief
laid it carefully
in the bottom of my trunk

2

I thought an ocean
between us
would muffle your voice
the waves were too quiet
the storms too infrequent

3

I went ashore
filled my ears
with the energy of America
rasping hammering cracking
    metal
saws biting into wood
picks and hammers into stone

In the moments
when the metal fell silent
every tree groaned as it
    fell
    separated
from its root
every rock
    protested
    split
apart at the fault

4

There were distractions:
cards at night in bunkhouses
    I upped my bets, couldn't lose
dances in Finntowns
    the insistent accordion
    the yielding women
    quick to my lead
    their bodies fine and fresh

Your voice faded to
an occasional whisper

There was one
I could have married
but her soul was too new
I left for Canada
promised to send for her
the words metal in my mouth

5

There was much to do alone
    clearing
    ploughing
    building
it was enough

Your letter came
tentative, ending with
a single roaring question—
shall I come?

6

When the train pulled in
you emerged from the steam
a solid black form
wrapped in layers, formless
a bundled child at each hand

The ride home:
twenty miles of silence
stars falling on the snow
I bedded in the oxen
you undressed the girls
we ate our first meal
bread, cheese, berry preserves
small chatter as a welcome
for your daughters
you spent a long time
putting them to bed

In the lamplight
I unwrapped
    you
unwrapped
    me
all my faults
your doubts
the seven years
fell away

New Finland, Canada
October 28, 1894

My dear father,

This is a letter to bless the day you were born. I wish
I could celebrate with you, eat berry preserves and
cake. I miss you, but I cannot say I'm lonely here in
this clump of Finns. They speak the same language
my tongue learned when my tongue was unlocked.
Sometimes the townspeople laugh at my English, but
I know enough to get along.

It is cold here today, nearing winter. But I'm used to
the cold: the same north wind, *pohjan tuuli,* blows
from Kauhava across the pole to Canada on our
huddle of buildings in Uusi Suomi. David shot a deer
this morning for the girls and me. He is bleeding and
gutting it, skinning its soft hide. He does it swiftly in
the barn, the cows shift and tremble in their stalls,
their eyes roll when they smell the blood. For a few
days their milk will be curdled, but soon they will
offer smooth milk again. The deer meat will be good.
David quarters it, hangs it in the *seppä* shop. It is
sweet and pungent and lean with the taste of wild
grass. He's a good man in my middle age.

> *What I must keep locked inside: Matt was seldom
> kind, though he struggled. You saw in his eyes
> what I could not see, tried to warn me. But why
> did you and mother close your door to me when I
> married him?*

The geese came down today from the north. David
ran in to tell me he heard them honking and growling
and filling the sky. He took me outside, we threw
back our heads, laughed and called to the geese. They
flew in a wide V from Vaasa, heading for warm islands.
David sings to me of the tropics, he went for a sailor
some of the years of his wandering. He ties up the horses
with sailors' knots, tells me stories in the *sauna.*

> *What I cannot ask you: why did mother hurt you?
> You never spoke harsh words in return, but
> charmed and teased her out of her moods.*

39

The girls are growing, they like David. He's carving
them dolls for Christmas. I wish they could see their
grandpa. I hope they marry men who love them, this
is a new land.

> David scrubs my back in the sauna
> tickles me with the vihta
> we throw cool water slowly
> on the hot stones
> prolonging the löyly
> the stones laugh with steam
> our bodies soften and ripen
> we go outside to cool off, recite the stars
> come in again for löyly
> After sauna, the house is quiet
> the girls are asleep in the loft
> we drink tea and look at each other
> make love as slowly as we can
> cool off and start again

We broke more land this year, 6 more acres. The crop
was healthy except for the oats, maybe we got some
bad seed. David has time now to build me a loom, the
rugs from Kauhava are finally wearing out. Take care
of yourself, do not worry about me, but write to me
again with news of Kauhava.

With love,
your goose, your girl,

Maria

PHOTOGRAPHER

I was the first woman photographer in the west
the one who captured women
their lined faces, tired eyes
children at their skirts
the ones buried in your trunks
whose names you don't remember

This one was Maria
she had eyes like the glint
of a bluebird's wing
fair hair braided and coiled
heavy as August wheat

Her dress that day was a clear red
if you look closely
you'll see tiny ovals on it
       little pointed eggs
       or grains of rice
in a flowing pattern

I posed her in front of the garden fence:
willow branches woven
into a landscape of hills
her daughters had gathered wild flowers
stuck them into the fence here and there

I caught her with one arm outstretched
beckoning to a wren

This is a picture of the girls
one was sprightly like her mother
the other tall and serious after her father
a study in contrasts

They helped me load the equipment into the buggy
it was cool in the house
I drank two dippers of cold spring water
many cups of strong coffee
with honey-dipped buns

When her husband came in from the field
I could see where her joy came from
if I'd ever met a man like that
I'd have packed up my camera and tripod
settled down on this flat prairie
and learned how to make honey buns

MARIA PRACTISES HER PART

Titania, mother of all
who have fallen in love with asses
you are here with Maria
teaching her your lines
from a notebook by lamplight
she translates as she reads:

> The moon, pale in her anger,
> washes all the air with her disease

This is indeed a wrong spring
snow on the budded willows
sprouted wheat frozen in the fields
anger among the neighbours
David, my Oberon, cool with me

If ever this clump of Finns
needed our midsummer play
our Juhannus bonfire burning all night
our dance until dawn
this is the year
our faces are dark
we need the fairy light

Maria goes out to the moon
says her lines from memory:

> And these small evils multiply
> through our complaint, our every argument

If I learn my part well
surely the audience will come together
laugh at me falling in love with an ass—
even the best of men
sometimes bray like a donkey
dumb as Bottom

She summons her helpers
Cobweb, Moth and Mustardseed:

> Lead my love to me, the moon is weeping
> tie up his tongue, bring him silently.

David returns, hide full of thorns
ears drooping, face long
but seeing moonlight on the log house
fireflies in the yard
he thinks of himself as Oberon

Titania sees him as Bottom
prepares a garland for his neck

HOW TO SURVIVE THE FUNERAL

Nod when they speak

then say thank you

Sing when the hymn begins

stop when it ends

close your eyes for the mumbling

open at amen

Look at your husband

he cannot look at you

NOW THAT DAVID IS GONE

Maria puts on his woolen pants
loose and scratchy on her legs
takes his rifle down to the pond
walks over the beaver dam
a bridge of clay and branches

It is dusk
she sits on a stone
the bark on the trees
has been gnawed
by hungry animals

A doe comes to drink
she raises the rifle
the doe stares up the barrel
through the peep-sight
Maria lowers the gun
she would like to see
the white tail of the doe
flickering up the hill
but David is gone, this is her job

She pulls the trigger twice
watches the doe crumple
when it is still
she kneels beside it
blesses its death, opens its neck

The blood of the doe spreads on the ground
flows into the darkening water
she knows the meat will be good

MARIA SEWS A WEDDING DRESS

With this needle
splinter of a reindeer bone
whittled and pierced
I sewed for you the tawny skin
of a southern deer
to wear on your wedding day

The treadle under my foot
guides the needle
through gathers of ivory lawn
that will billow out
from the sinews of your waist

My dress when I married your father
was heavy and black
in the old style of the *vanha maa*
tight at the throat
I wore a crown of brass filigree
polished bright as gold

May you be blessed with a daughter
as wild and bright as you
the deer we saw in the forest
gazing down the hillside

If I ever marry again
I will weave the linen myself
the fit will be loose
I will walk barefoot
through the wolf willow
to the bottom of the hill
and all the guests will be strangers

MARIA AND THE CHILDREN

Walking home from the stone church
Ruusa and Mikko time their steps
little Juha trails behind
pulling a stick in the hot dust

No rain for three summers
the pastor says we all must pray
for God to take the curse off the land
force the sinners to repent
the drinkers to dry up
let the rain fall again

Juha is learning his Finnish letters
from the pastor's *aapinen*
he draws them in the dust

    a is for *aamu* this is the morning
    a is for *aurinko* here is the sun
    e is for *emakko* this is a mama pig
    e is for *eukko* here's the old woman

Let's visit the old woman
eukko Maria, I like her stories
better than the pastor's
she lets us pet her pig
gives us sun cookies
dusted with sugar

Maria sings of heroes and magic:
Ilmarinen, who forged the Sampo
    source of all riches, grain, and salt
Lemminkäinen, who bridled the devil's elk
    to woo the witch's daughter
Aino, who drowned in the sea
    rather than marry the old wizard
Väinämöinen, who chanted the rocks alive
    sang himself out of a giant's belly

Maria, can Väinämöinen sing back the rain?
Was he your husband in Finland?
I'm not that old, chickens, ancient as I am
Väinämöinen was there when the world began:

    Kauan sitten, long ago
    Ilmatar, goddess of air
    floated in emptiness
    the wind blew upon her
    conceived a child
    for seven hundred years she groaned
    waiting to give birth

    She created the sea as a resting place
    floated on the waves
    till a bird with golden eyes nested in her lap
    laid seven eggs and brooded them
    Ilmatar twitched and they fell in the sea
    the bits of shell, the spots of yolk and white
    made heavens and earth
    stars and moon, mountains and lakes

    The name of her son was Väinämöinen
    born an old man in midst of the waves
    he swam to shore and searched for a wife
    for six, seven years he searched for a wife
    but his back was so stooped, his hair so white
    that no young bride would have him
    From the jaw of a pike he made a kantele
    sang to console himself, sang to heal
    first of singers, he gave us joy

The children are playing a game in the barn
you be Ilmatar, I'll be the wizard
Juha can be the golden-eyed bird
Ilmatar lies on a sea of straw
the bird brings seven eggs for her skirt
she twitches and jumps, they fall and break
Ilmatar flings the shells around
creates the mountains and lakes

Their father, Jaakob, sees his daughter
flinging worlds about as if she were God
sees her stretched out on the hay
sees her brother crawl out from between her legs
he hobbles and leans on a crooked stick:
    No wonder my back is bent
    all that time locked up in your belly
    Ilmatar, mother of all the world
    I shall sing for my birth as the first of men

My children, what blasphemy is this?
Are you forgetting the Bible,
Adam and Eve, God the Father?
    Oh, no, that happened too. Maria told us
    but I like Ilmatar, goddess of wind
    better than the fierce old God
    the pastor yells at us about
I'll teach you about God, you little pagans!

Jaakob imprints his God
with a leather horse whip
on his children's bare legs.
Now say thank you and go to your chores.
I'll have a word with that Maria.

MIDWIFE

The *sauna* is the best place for a birth
warm as a womb
I used to sit on a bed of towels
on the lowest shelf
waiting and thinking
how would this baby be?
I looked at the knots in the wood
watched the flame in the lantern

Finally Maria would arrive:
    How come you get an old woman
    out of her warm cosy bed?
    Oh well, now that I'm here
    let's see if there's a little one hiding

She sang as she stroked
my belly, legs, back
loosening the skin and nerves
she wiped my face with cool water
made circles with her fingertips
on my forehead and temples
her hands were rough from work
she wasn't afraid to use pressure

When the time came near she crouched below me
kneading and stretching the walls
every time the pain bore down
the *sauna* walls contracted
she told me to throw my pain
into the water, throw it on the stones
let it steam away

She had a chant for breathing:
   Yksi, kaksi, wind goes in
   kolme, neljä, hold it there
   viisi, kuusi, shoo it out
Another verse when she saw the baby's head:
   Open up, my flower
   come out, my bird
   don't be afraid to leave your nest

When the baby came she caught it
cradled it, cleaned away the blood
laid it on my chest
I closed my eyes
saw a lake, a sunrise,
maybe a rainbow or northern lights
heard music on the shore
like a soft flute, *huhuilua*
We floated and rested on the waves
Maria rowed us back to shore

MARIA MAKES SOAP

1

Eukko sika, witch of a sow
I nursed you as a runt
now you trample the young of your young
with your wicked old hoofs!

> She's killed pigs before
> but this one's too mean
> and Maria knows she's getting old

> Hitching her skirts above her boots
> she strides off through the snow
> to the neighbour Lauttamus
> to fetch young Gus the smith
> he has a way with animals
> treated the sow last week
> for running sores in her eyes

> Old Juha is splitting wood
> his axe true, his forearms thick
> when he sees Maria
> his back straightens
> like a sapling slowly released
> but she heads straight for the *seppä* shop
> without so much as *päivä*
> for the friend of her youth

My son has gone to Yorkton
he won't be back for a week
come in for a coffee—what's the matter?

The old sow's gone crazy
needs to be put down
can you do the job?

Can I do the job? Do you see that woodpile?

> Never mind his years
> Juha is up for the task
> still on the green side of fourscore
> if he can kill the sow clean
> maybe Maria will listen to him
> she always says
> they're both too old to marry

2

Maria is making soap
she skims the clean fat
from the rendering pot
the rotten silt settles on the bottom
she thinks how good it is
to be so useful after you're gone:
haunches into salt pork
thick skin for tanning
gallons of fat for soap

But this old sow's fat
reeks of bitterness
I'd better not add too much lye
or I'll burn the sheets when I boil them

3

Juha's a fine man for his age
he skiied both here and back
the red tassel flying on his hat
he killed the old sow clean
with just one hammer blow

Perhaps I'll consider his offer
I've had two husbands, do I need a third?
But he makes me laugh, warms my blood
I've known him all my life
he's a strong man and a good man
with the notions of a young man

It's time to heat the *sauna*, think it over
maybe if I use this soap
my skin will crack off
I'll be a newborn piglet underneath

Guess I'm not ready yet
for the rendering pot

IDENTITIES————

KANADALAINEN

To have left behind the language
that flowed like spring water
the easy seepage
of fresh words every hour

To have come to a land
of thorough drought
with a dry tongue

To have to pump the handle
like a child again
lifted off the platform
by every upstroke
the pump so stiff
the well so dark
you doubt the alkali earth
will ever release its sour water

To hang a new pail
from the knuckle
on the pump mouth
watching the water trickle
slowly at first
then slowly faster
until the pail is overflowing,
only to stumble on a root
on the path to the house

To watch the pumped water
settle and seep
into insatiable
Canadian earth

To have believed the words
would ever flow together
into sentences

HOW TO SAY "MARIA"

"Maria"—say it with the accent
heavy on the "Ma,"
make the "r"
a soft half-whistle
on the tongue tip
a suggestion
of vibration,
slip off the end of her name
with a quick fall—"Maria"

Listen to her voice:
roam with me, says Maria
we will find berries
they are *marjat*
there is room here in my cottage
rest with me, says Maria
we will make *piirakat*
with rye flour and rice filling
come to me
   rakas nainen
   loved woman
I will rock you
   raskas nainen
   melancholy woman

MARJAT/MARIA

I am searching for berries
mustikoita
mansikoita
karpaloita
but the picking is slow
all the blueberries
have been blackened by drought
into dried bits of grit
the strawberries are all seed
the cranberries sparse and hard

Motley berries rattle in my pail
as I pass the slough
on the way to my grandmother's
pockmarks of hoofprints
are dried into the mud edges
like crackled sepia photographs
smudged by ink-blots

This isn't the year for berries
maybe it's the year for poems

MARIA'S WILL

When Maria died she left me
her *koivukoru* filled with runes
on horns of cattle
razors bright as silver
edged with healing
leather thongs
to bind bones

    She makes feathery slits
    where the blood collects
    on the back of my neck
    across my shoulders
    the base of my spine
    applies the horns
    they grasp my back
    a surgical suction
    in patterns of curves

    The blackness flows
    which she draws to her lips
    till the cups are full
    she empties each horn
    into the fire
    the flames turn black
    the smell of my fears
    fills the room

    She reads the smoke
    translates it to memories
    I dare not claim
    till her words convince me
    and I am healed

TALISMAN

A talisman, once chosen
can never be discarded
hers is a single cow bone
picked up in a prairie field
a casual treasure

one grey vertebra
        separate
whose patterns of curves and holes
show as weathered wings
        held up to the sky
show as a hollow face
        reflected in a glass table

this bone accompanies her
in places she lives
        houses, rooms
sometimes it is on the bookshelf
sometimes beside her bed
        next to the lamp
sometimes on the back of stove
        where it plays a tune
        she sings

this bone has become these years
all that is blown clean by wind
        when she walks outside
all that is hidden in the body
        when she crouches alone

if you want to know her
look at the bone:
        animal
        air
        earth
        flower
        spine

ACKNOWLEDGEMENTS

Some of these poems have been broadcast on CBC Radio's "Alberta Anthology" and the Finnish Radio Broadcasting Corporation; performed at "Womanstrength" (sponsored by Celebration of Women in the Arts); and published in *Canadian Forum, Canadian Woman Studies/les cahiers de la femme, NeWest Review, Northward Journal, Other Voices, Prism International*, and the anthology *Sampo: The Magic Mill* (Minneapolis: New Rivers Press, 1989).

I am grateful to the Alberta Foundation for the Literary Arts for a travel and writing grant, and to the Suomi College Finnish Archives in Hancock, Michigan, for research assistance. My special thanks to the people of New Finland, Saskatchewan; Hannah Martin, one of Maria's granddaughters; Michael Shields, *avomies*; and all my literary midwives, especially Earle Birney, Bert Almon, Leona Gom, and the members of my writing group.

COTEAU BOOKS

Coteau Books is an imprint of Thunder Creek Publishing Co-operative, a non-profit press established in 1975 to publish Canadian literature. For a complete catalogue of poetry, fiction, plays, criticism and children's titles, please write to Box 239, Substation #1, Moose Jaw, Saskatchewan S6H 5V0.

POETRY FROM COTEAU BOOKS

Allen, Elizabeth, *Territories.* A second collection from Allen. Her terrain is the Saskatchewan rural landscape, given distinctive treatment. $6.00 pbk. Fall 1984.

Buckaway, Catherine M., *Blue Windows.* Poetry with lyric elegance from a prolific writer. $8.00 pbk/$16.00 cl. Fall 1988.

Burrs, Mick, *The Blue Pools of Paradise.* A poignant collection of wide-ranging poetry. $6.00 pbk. Fall 1983.

Cooley, Dennis, *Perishable Light.* New poems from an accomplished poet and scholar. $8.00 pbk/$16.00 cl. Spring 1988.

Crozier, Lorna and Gary Hyland, editors, *A Sudden Radiance: Saskatchewan Poetry.* The first release in the Carlyle King Anthology Series; a comprehensive collection of work by established poets. $14.95 pbk/$21.95 cl. Fall 1987.

Crozier, Lorna, *The Weather.* Vibrant and beautiful poetry by an accomplished poet. $6.00 pbk. Fall 1983.

Dyck, E.F., *Odpoems &.* Dyck's first collection of poems, featuring the strange adventures of Od. $4.00 pbk. Fall 1978.

Geddes, Gary, *Changes of State.* Powerful, arresting poetry by an internationally acclaimed poet. $7.00 pbk/$15.00 cl. Spring 1986.

Gruending, Dennis, *Gringo: Poems and Journals from Latin America.* Accessible, powerful poetry chronicling Gruending's experiences in Latin America. $6.00 pbk. Spring 1983.

Hillis, Rick, *The Blue Machines of Night.* The seventh volume in the Wood Mountain Series of new poets. $8.00 pbk/$16.00 cl. Spring 1988.

Hyland, Gary, *Street of Dreams.* Hyland's themes are found within his own community and are treated with charm and grace. $7.00 pbk. Spring 1984.

Kerr, Don, *Going Places*. Poetry that explores the delights of family motoring on the prairie. $6.00 pbk. Fall 1983.

Kerr, Don and Anne Szumigalski, editors, *Heading Out: The New Saskatchewan Poets*. A sparkling collection of work by Saskatchewan's newer poets. $9.95 pbk/$15.95 cl. Fall 1986.

Krause, Judith, *What We Bring Home*. Second in the Wood Mountain Series. Well-crafted poetry from a new poet. $7.00 pbk/$15.00 cl. Spring 1986.

Mattson, Nancy, *Maria Breaks Her Silence*. A poetic biography of a Finnish immigrant. Ninth in the Wood Mountain Series. $8.00 pbk/$21.95 cl. Spring 1989.

McLean, Jim, *The Secret Life of Railroaders*. The funniest poems ever to roll down the main line. $5.00 pbk. Fall 1982.

Morrissey, Kim, *Batoche*. A series of poems on the North West Resistance of 1885. Eighth in the Wood Mountain Series. $8.00 pbk/$21.95 cl. Spring 1989.

Poirier, Thelma and Jean Hillabold, *Double Visions*. The first book in the Wood Mountain Series, this collection introduces two Saskatchewan women poets. $6.00 pbk/$14.00 cl. Fall 1984.

Robertson, William B., *Standing On Our Own Two Feet*. Third in the Wood Mountain Series, now in its second printing. Poems that speak of everyday experiences. $7.00 pbk/$15.00 cl. Fall 1987.

Rush, Jerry, *Earth Dreams*. Startling images and tightly controlled lyrics reveal new perspectives. $5.00 pbk. Fall 1982.

St. George, Elyse Yates, *White Lions in the Afternoon*. Sixth in the Wood Mountain Series. A book of poetry and visual art. $7.00 pbk/$15.00 cl. Fall 1987.

Sorestad, Glen, *Hold the Rain in Your Hands: Poems New & Selected*. Clear, accessible poetry — the best from five earlier collections plus 29 new poems. $8.95 pbk/$15.95 cl. Spring 1985.

Wilson, Paul, *The Fire Garden*. Fifth in the Wood Mountain Series. A collection of new poetry on a wide range of contemporary themes. $7.00 pbk/$15.00 cl. Spring 1987.

Nancy Mattson is a third-generation Finnish Canadian. She spent all of her childhood summers on her grandparents' homesteads in New Finland, Saskatchewan. *Maria Breaks Her Silence* is Nancy's first book of poetry on the Finnish immigrants' experiences, but she has written several articles and edited a local history on the subject, *Life in the New Finland Woods: A History of New Finland, Saskatchewan* (1982). Nancy has travelled to Finland as an invited speaker on Canadian literature by and about Finnish Canadians.

Nancy's poetry has appeared in many Canadian periodicals, including *Prism International, Canadian Forum, NeWest Review, Canadian Woman Studies/ les cahiers de la femme* and *Capilano Review*, and in the anthology of Finnish American writing, *Sampo: The Magic Mill* (1989). Several of the poems in this collection have been aired on CBC Radio's "Alberta Anthology."

Nancy holds a Master of Arts in English. She lives in Edmonton and works as an editor at the University of Alberta.